EARLY THEMES

Colors

Ready-to-Go Activities, Games,
Literature Selections, Poetry, and Everything
You Need for a Complete Theme Unit

by Courtney Silk

SCHOLASTIC
PROFESSIONAL BOOKS

NEW YORK • TORONTO • LONDON • AUCKLAND • SYDNEY

I am eternally grateful to Bill, Mom, Dad, Stacy, Kelly and Sam
for their endless support, encouragement, and assistance.
Without you there would be no color in my world.
Many thanks to my editor Joan Novelli for your patience and guidance.

Edited by Joan Novelli
Cover design by Vincent Ceci and Jaime Lucero
Cover art by Jo Lynn Alcorn
Interior design by Solutions by Design, Inc.
Interior illustration by Abby Carter

ISBN 0-590-13270-9

Contents

About this Book

From the time they are born, children experience the colors in their world—reacting at first to black and white, then to the wide range of colors that become part of their lives. Children are naturally drawn to colors—from the foods they choose to the clothes they wear, the toys they reach for, the early art they create, and the trees, birds, and other life outside their windows. *Early Themes: Colors* invites students to take a closer look at the colors in their world, beginning with something they're very familiar with—their own eyes.

Children move on to explore the science of colors, discover how artists use colors (and experiment with their techniques), investigate the way colorful traffic signs help people stay safe, learn how mapmakers, bakers, and other workers use color in their jobs, and more. Like a magnifying glass to their world, *Early Themes: Colors* is designed to encourage children to make connections, build understanding of key concepts, and view their world from a fresh and more detailed perspective.

WHAT'S INSIDE

Think of this book as a toolbox for teaching and learning. The material is entirely flexible—you can use the activities and ideas as they appear or adapt them to create a customized unit on color. Among the tools you'll find inside are:

◎ Color Scavenger Hunt (an interactive poster);

◎ suggested professional resources;

◎ strategies for setting up a bright, appealing learning center, and Learning Center Links throughout the book to keep your center going strong;

◎ introductory activities to motivate children's thinking about color;

◎ step-by-step lesson frameworks for cross-curricular, interactive activities and experiments;

◎ background information, extensions, and Literature Connections to complement lessons;

◎ age-appropriate reproducibles, including a mini-book to make;

◎ festive wrap-up activities to celebrate children's experiences.

WHY TEACH WITH THEMES?

Teaching with themes has many benefits—for both teacher and child. Building a unit around a topic that is part of children's lives inspires curiosity and motivates learning. Theme teaching also provides a framework for an integrated curriculum, encouraging children to make meaningful connections in different subject areas as they learn. When children can select and connect information from different curriculum areas, they also demonstrate their potential for being creative and analytical thinkers—a skill with lifelong benefits.

By focusing on fewer topics in greater depth, themes help children avoid information overload and enjoy and appreciate the learning process. As they explore a theme in depth, children have many opportunities to revisit concepts over time, building on their understanding and increasing retention.

For teachers, theme teaching is a convenient way to structure lessons and organize the day. Whether it's a hands-on science experiment you're setting up or a math activity you're planning, you'll find that one activity naturally leads to another—making it easy to weave subject areas into your day in a meaningful way. For example, as children investigate eye color in the classroom, they'll also graph and interpret results, combining science with math and language arts. Literacy development is woven throughout—with children reading, writing, speaking, and listening for a purpose.

BEFORE YOU BEGIN

Here are some suggestions to help plan your unit.

Materials

While most of the lessons call for readily available materials, it may be helpful to read through the list before you begin any activity to determine if there are additional supplies you might need. Make a list of what's missing and check with your school, parents, and others to see what you can get together. With a little advance planning, you may find that between what you have on hand and what others are willing to donate, you can pull your materials together at no cost.

Home-School Connection

Send a letter home to share news about your theme unit. Include a request for materials and volunteers. Think about continuing the newsletter throughout the unit, updating parents on what their children are learning, sharing samples of student work and suggesting ways families can extend learning at home.

Grouping

Many of the lessons suggest grouping children—a strategy that helps ensure an organized working environment in which every child can make a contribution. You might like to set up groups at the onset so children can delve right into the lessons with a minimum of preparation. Children can select color names for their groups and design colorful banners that include the group's name and the names of its members.

Assessment

A portfolio of children's work is a helpful assessment tool. It is also a special keepsake for children. Students can use file folders, folders with pockets, boxes—even large pieces of construction paper folded in half and taped at the sides. Have them write their names on their portfolios and add theme-specific stickers, stamps, drawings, and other decorations. As children complete activities and projects, they'll have a handy place to keep everything together.

Color Check

Can all of your students see colors? This is an important piece of information to know before beginning this unit. Color-vision deficit or color-perception alteration (more commonly referred to as color blindness) is a partial or complete inability to tell colors apart. It is common in about 7 percent of males and 0.5 percent of females. There are several kinds of tests that screen for this—children may have been tested during routine eye exams at school. If you have concerns about any of your students, check their health records or speak with the school nurse or physician.

SETTING UP A LEARNING CENTER

A *Colors* learning center, though not necessary for the activities in this book, can be an exciting addition to your theme. Centers enhance learning in many ways.

Some of the things learning centers can do for you and your students include:

◎ act as a visual focal point for a theme and motivate interest and participation;

◎ allow all students to become involved in the theme by providing opportunities to work in groups as well as independently;

◎ provide a stimulating work area for children who want to know more and can independently explore on their own;

◎ encourage children to assist one another in various ways, giving each student a chance to shine;

◎ provide a central location for storing and displaying theme materials and long-term projects.

Here's a plan for creating a *Colors* learning center in your classroom.

1 Set up a work space that includes a table, several chairs, and a wall space. Invite children to help decorate the center with pictures and projects they create throughout the unit. Students can display their group banners here too. (See Grouping, page 5.)

2 Organize assorted art supplies, including paper, markers, crayons, paint, clay, colored cellophane, tissue paper, scissors, and glue. Shoe boxes or baskets come in handy for storing materials.

3 Provide colored manipulatives and containers for sorting.

4 Display the Color Scavenger Hunt poster. (See pullout.) Add word webs, graphs, and charts as the class completes them. A color wheel is a worthwhile addition too.

5 Gather assorted reading materials, such as:

◎ children's literature (see Literature Connections throughout the book for suggestions);

◎ related reading materials children bring from home.

6 Use the center as an activity hub. Look for Learning Center Links throughout the book to keep activities fresh.

Professional Resources

Exploring Art Masterpieces with Young Learners: Pull-out Posters of Four Great Works with Hands-on Activities Across the Curriculum by Rhonda Graff Silver (Scholastic Professional Books, 1997). Contains biographies of famous artists, poster-sized reproductions of their work, and related activities.

Graphing Across the Curriculum by Valerie Williams and Tina Cohen (Scholastic Professional Books, 1995). Ideas for all kinds of graphs.

Kids' Crazy Concoctions: 50 Mysterious Mixtures for Art & Craft Fun by Jill Frankel Hauser (Williamson, 1995). This exceptional book mixes information about how to create art materials with interesting facts.

Learning Centers: Getting Them Started, Keeping Them Going by Michael F. Opitz (Scholastic Professional Books, 1994). Everything you need to know about how to make learning centers a part of your classroom.

Paint Adventures by Kathy Savage-Hubbard and Rose C. Speicher (North Light Books, 1993). Simple projects that use common household materials.

Picture This: A First Introduction to Paintings by Felicity Woolf (Doubleday, 1989). Famous works from major periods of art history introduce children to Western paintings dating from 1400 to 1950.

The Pocket Chart Book by Valerie Schiffer Danoff (Scholastic Professional Books, 1996). How-to ideas for using pocket charts across the curriculum; useful for many of the *Colors* theme activities.

Science Arts: Discovering Science Through Art Experiences by Mary Ann Kohl and Jean Potter (Bright Ring Publishing, 1993). Explore basic science concepts through art activities.

Science Crafts for Kids: 50 Fantastic Things to Invent and Create by Gwen Diehn and Terry Krautwurst (Sterling Publishing, 1994). Engaging, interactive experiments and activities, including several on colors.

When Blue Meant Yellow: How Colors Got Their Names by Jeanne Heifetz (Henry Holt and Company, 1994). This is a must-have, with extensive information on the origins of color.

OTHER

Binney & Smith, the maker of Crayola Crayons, offers a variety of educational materials. For more information, call (800) CRAYOLA.

LAUNCHING THE THEME:

Color in My World

In building a fitting foundation to a unit on colors, children begin their explorations with something they know best—their own eye color! With these introductory activities, they will investigate eye color, use their eyes to solve color riddles, and explore what color means to them through poetry and art. If you're setting up a learning center, this is a good time to plan an orientation to introduce your students to the area and activities. The Learning Center Links on page 11 suggest activities to get you started.

My Eyes, Your Eyes

Children determine which eye color is the most prevalent among their classmates then graph the results.

Materials

- ◎ mural paper
- ◎ chart paper
- ◎ mirrors
- ◎ 3-by-5-inch slips of white paper (or index cards)
- ◎ crayons, markers

Greens Hazel Brown

Teaching the Lesson

1. Divide a sheet of mural paper into seven vertical columns. Beginning at the bottom of the second column from the left, write the name of a different eye color (blue, violet, green, hazel, brown, and black) in each column. To assist children in word recognition, color-code these labels. Display at a child's eye level.

2. Invite children to predict which color eyes most of their classmates will have.

Record their predictions on chart paper.

3. Have children take turns looking in a mirror to identify the color of their eyes. Then let them choose a crayon that most closely matches that color and use it to draw a picture of their eyes on a slip of paper. Have children write their names on the slips.

4. Ask children to come up to the mural paper with their pictures and form lines in front of the color word that matches their eye color.

5. Elicit children's observations about the length of each line. Now which eye color do they think is most common in their class?

6. Have children tape their slips of paper in the appropriate columns on the mural paper. Together, count how many slips of paper there are in each column.

7. At the bottom of the first column (left blank), write the number zero. At the top of the column, write the highest total for any one eye-color column. Fill in the numbers in between at the top of each column and have children compare the totals for each color with their predictions.

 ACTIVITY Extension Let children work in pairs or groups to create story problems based on information in the graph. For example: Five children have green eyes. We have 20 children in our class. How many children don't have green eyes? Display the story problems around the mural for children to solve.

 Literature Connection Extend children's understanding of the way eyes work by sharing these books.

Seeing Things by Alan Fowler (Children's Press, 1991)

One Eye, Two Eyes, Three Eyes, Four: The Many Ways Animals See by Dorothy Leon (Messner, 1980)

Eyes by Judith Worthy (Doubleday, 1988)

LANGUAGE ARTS

What Is Pink?

Children create a mural that shows what colors represent to them.

Materials

◎ mural paper

◎ reproducible poem (see page 13)

◎ markers, crayons, paint

◎ drawing paper

◎ tape

◎ magazines (optional)

Teaching the Lesson

1. Divide the mural paper into six large sections. At the top of each section, write *What is _____?* Fill in the blank for each section with a different color. For example, What is pink? What is red? What is green? What is yellow? and so on. (Use marker or crayon in the color noted to provide visual clues for reading.) Place the mural paper in an open space on the floor.

2. Read the poem "What Is Pink?," by Christina Rossetti, with children several times. You may want to copy it onto chart paper so they can follow along. Ask: Why do you think the author chose the objects she did to represent colors?

3. Gather children around the mural paper. With them, read the questions at the top of each section. Invite children to draw or cut out pictures from magazines to show what each of the colors means to them. Before they begin, you may want to give them some quiet tim͜ ͜ think about what they would like to draw.

4. Let children visit the mural in small groups to add their pictures. Help children gain an appreciation of one another's ideas by talking about the different ways they chose to represent each color.

ACTIVITY Extension Once the mural is complete, let children compose their own poems (or a class poem) about colors, using Christina Rossetti's as a model. Let children know that their words do not have to rhyme. Have children illustrate their poems, then frame on construction paper for a display. Or, bind the pages with an O-ring to make a class poetry anthology.

Literature Connection Share *Nicky's Walk* by Cathryn Falwell (Clarion, 1991), then take children for a walk outside so they, too, can name colors they see.

Color Scavenger Hunt

Children have fun solving riddles on the Color Scavenger Hunt poster and create their own color posters with riddles for classmates to solve.

Materials

- Color Scavenger Hunt poster (bound in back)
- magazines
- construction paper
- glue
- scissors

Teaching the Lesson

1. Display the poster on a wall and invite children to gather around it and share observations.

2. Read aloud the riddle on the poster and invite children to solve it—quietly at first so that everyone has a chance to discover the hidden objects.

3. Now let children create their own Color Scavenger Hunt picture riddles. Distribute construction paper, magazines, scissors, and glue. Have children look through the magazines and cut out pictures of about 10 to 20 different-color objects then arrange them on the construction paper to make a picture.

4. Once children have finished their pictures, have them use the riddle on the poster as a model for composing their own riddles. Put riddles and pictures together to make a book to share at your learning center. Set up a schedule for children to share the book at home too.

ACTIVITY Extension Challenge children to a colors-in-the-room scavenger hunt. For example, you might have them find three objects that represent each color, then draw pictures on a record sheet to show what they found. Children will have fun creating their own color scavenger hunts to share too.

Literature Connection Children who enjoy hidden picture riddles will enjoy pouring over books in the *I Spy* series, with riddles by Jean Marzollo and photographs by Walter Wick (Scholastic). Challenge them to find unusual ways that Walter uses objects in his settings. For example, in *I Spy Spooky Night*, clothespins are made to look like a fence around a flower bed.

Learning Center Link

Have children write more riddles to go with the art on the Color Scavenger Hunt poster. Display them around the poster for new challenges.

What Is Pink?

by Christina Rossetti

What is pink? A rose is pink
By the fountain's brink.
What is red? A poppy's red
In its barley bed.
What is blue? The sky is blue
Where the clouds float through.
What is white? A swan is white
Sailing in the light.
What is yellow? Pears are yellow,
Rich and ripe and mellow.
What is green? The grass is green,
With small flowers between.
What is violet? Clouds are violet
In the summer twilight.
What is orange? Why, an orange,
Just an orange!

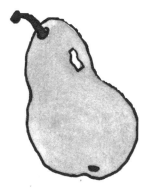

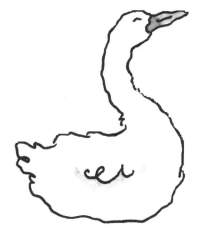

Our Color Lab

With the hands-on activities in this section, children become color scientists—gathering and interpreting data about favorite colors, exploring the way colors come together, experimenting with the way the sun acts on sandpaper prints, investigating patterns in rainbows, and more.

SCIENCE NOTES

Light looks as if it has no color but it is actually made up of all of the colors of the rainbow. When light reaches the eye, the eye mixes all of the greens, blues, and reds and sees only white. The eye sees certain colors in objects because of dyes and pigments in those objects. Dyes and pigments absorb some of the colors in white light and reflect back others.

Color By Numbers

Children vote to determine the class's favorite color then create charts and graphs to illustrate their findings.

Materials

◎ mural paper

◎ 3-by-5-inch index cards

◎ crayons

◎ tape

Teaching the Lesson

1 Divide mural paper into columns. Write various color names as headings at the top of each column. This will be your color tracker. Display it on a wall or on the chalkboard.

2 Begin by asking: What do you think most children in our class would say is their favorite color? Record their predictions on chart paper or on the chalkboard.

3 Let children know that they will find out what the favorite color is by taking a vote. Then have children write the name of their favorite color on an index card (or use a crayon to scribble the color).

4 Invite children to take turns taping their cards under the corresponding color columns on the color tracker.

5 Together, count aloud the total number of cards in each column. Record the totals at the top of each column. Elicit children's conclusions about the results by asking questions such as: Which color is the class's favorite? How do you know this?

6 Have children form color groups in front of the color tracker (sitting in a line in front of the color for which they voted). Challenge children with questions that require them to use the information they've gathered, such as: Do more people like blue or red? How many more people like green than yellow? Were any colors not chosen? What is Keisha's favorite color? Is it the same as Michael's? Is this the color you predicted? Do you think the results would be the same for the class next door? For the school? How could we test our predictions?

7 Work with children to create a graph that illustrates their findings. (See Graph Grab Bag, page 17.)

ACTIVITY Extension Plan a "Come in Colors!" Day with your students. Children can dress from head to toe in a favorite color. Play color-related games such as color tag and red rover.

Literature Connection The class in *Red Day, Green Day* by Edith Kunhardt (Greenwillow, 1992) is also learning about colors. This book is a perfect introduction to the Color Lab activities. Other books to share include *I Want to Paint My Bathroom Blue* by Ruth Krauss (HarperCollins, 1956) and *Red Is Best* by Kathy Stinson (Firefly, 1992).

GRAPH GRAB BAG

◎ On mural paper, create a bar graph that ranks favorite colors from most to least favorite. Write the number of students on the vertical axis and the colors on the horizontal axis. Let children shade in the graph to show how many votes each color received.

◎ Design a graph that illustrates which color each child selected as his or her favorite. Lay a large piece of mural paper on a table or on the floor. Along the vertical axis of the graph, write each color name. Along the horizontal axis, have each child write his or her name. Ask children to draw and cut out index-card size pictures of themselves. Then have children take turns pointing to their names on the graph. Direct children to start at their names and move their fingers up the graph until they come to the row with their favorite color. Have children paste their pictures in the spot where their finger is resting.

Learning Center Link

Display a variety of manipulatives such as pattern blocks, beads, and Cuisenaire Rods for color patterning activities. Children can take turns starting color patterns for classmates to continue.

Mystery Mix-Ups

Children experiment with combining primary colors to create secondary colors.

Materials (for each pair)

◎ record sheet (see page 22)

◎ red, yellow, and blue food coloring (place a few drops of each into paper cups)

◎ three eyedroppers

◎ shaving cream

◎ four reclosable sandwich bags

◎ finger-paint paper

Teaching the Lesson

1 Introduce the concepts of primary and secondary colors. Explain that red, yellow and blue are called *primary colors*. When the primary colors are mixed together in different ways, they make new colors. These are called *secondary colors*. The secondary colors are orange, violet or purple, and green.

17

2. Divide children into pairs. Have each pair pick up a set of materials, including a record sheet, four reclosable sandwich bags, individual paper cups of red, blue, and yellow food coloring, three eyedroppers (or have children share bottles or tubes of food coloring to eliminate the need for eyedroppers and paper cups).

3. Demonstrate how to mix one of the color combinations listed on the record sheet: Squirt shaving cream into a reclosable bag. Place a few drops of each color into the bag—one color to the left, the other to the right. Seal the bag. Ask: What color do you think I will make if I squish these two together? Stop here so that you don't reveal the secondary color.

Note: *Yellow food coloring may look red or orange when it is first squeezed out of the bottle.*

4. Let children continue by making predictions for each color equation on the record sheet then mixing the color combinations one at a time to discover the new colors. As children work, have them fill in the record sheet to show their results. How do their predictions compare?

5. Let children use their secondary-color shaving cream to finger paint.

ACTIVITY Extension
Sit with children in a circle. Pass around several crayons with unusual names. Discuss why the crayon makers may have chosen the different names. Then give children an opportunity to invent and name new colors. (Some food color packaging features a color blending chart on the back. Children can use this chart as inspiration.) Invite children to write or dictate stories about how they chose names for their new colors. Display their stories with swatches of the colors they invented.

Literature Connection

Three delightful books about color mixing, sure to inspire children's inventiveness, are:

Mouse Paint by Ellen Stoll Walsh (Harcourt Brace Jovanovich, 1989). Three white mice discover jars of red, blue, and yellow paint and create new colors. As you read this story to children, ask them to guess which color will be created each time the mice mix new paints.

Little Blue and Little Yellow by Leo Lionni (Mulberry Books, 1992). When two spots—one blue, one yellow—hug each other, they become green. Children will enjoy making up their own stories about spots of color after they read this book.

Color Dance by Ann Jonas (Greenwillow Books, 1989). Three dancers show how colors combine. After reading this story with children, let them do a color dance of their own by finger painting to music.

Learning Center Link

Let children explore color-mixing on their own by making spoon-and-smoosh paintings. Provide paper, spoons, and finger paints. Have children spoon paints onto their papers, fold, rub, and open. What new colors did they make?

Sun Prints

Children explore color and texture by creating sandpaper prints—with a little help from the sun.

Materials

- ◎ sandpaper
- ◎ old crayons
- ◎ construction paper or plain paper
- ◎ coins

Note: *You might want to tie this activity into an area of study in your classroom. For example, if you're studying the sea, children can create pictures of ocean life then put their finished prints together to create a mural or other display.*

Teaching the Lesson

1. Distribute sandpaper and crayons for children to create their sandpaper prints. Invite children to color on the sandpaper, for example, creating a design or a picture. Suggest that children bear down hard on their crayons as they color.

2. Have children place their sandpaper pictures on a sunny windowsill. Visit the windowsill periodically to observe and discuss changes. (The crayon will begin to melt.) This is a good time to talk about ways we use the sun's warmth.

3. Once the crayon warms up, invite a child to demonstrate how to place paper over the sandpaper drawing and rub the back of the paper hard with a coin. An imprint of the design will be transferred onto their paper. Have the other children make prints of their own pictures and display.

ACTIVITY Extension Put crayon shavings into a muffin tin, one color per cup. Put the tin on a warming tray until the crayon melts. Let the crayon cool a bit, then have children dip cotton swabs in and paint designs on oak tag or cardboard.

Literature Connection Learn more about the sun's warm ways with *Sun Song*, by Jean Marzollo (HarperCollins, 1995), a story told in image-rich verse.

Learning Center Link

Display other print-making materials for children to experiment with this art form. For example, they can use the tip of a paintbrush to etch designs into foam trays, then paint over, and print on paper. If you have Wikki-Stix (sticky, colorful strips of string, available in toy and craft stores), children can use the strips to create designs on paper, then lightly coat the raised area with paint to make prints.

What Makes a Rainbow?

You don't have to wait for a rain shower to investigate rainbows. With this activity, children make their own rainbows to explore the science behind this colorful light show, including the color pattern of a rainbow.

SCIENCE NOTES

Rainbows are arc-shaped bands of color. A rainbow usually appears during or after a lateday rain shower when the sun is shining. Rainbows are formed when sunlight shines through water droplets. The water splits the sunlight into different colors before it reaches us. A rainbow has seven colors. Beginning with the outer curve, they are red, orange, yellow, green, blue, indigo and violet. A helpful way for children to remember the color pattern of a rainbow is the acronym ROY G BIV. This acronym is formed by the first letter of every color of the rainbow.

Materials

◎ drawing paper

◎ crayons

◎ chart paper

◎ a 1-quart or 1-liter clear glass jar

◎ white poster board

Teaching the Lesson

1 Introduce the activity by asking each child to draw a picture of a rainbow.

2 As a group, compare and contrast the pictures. Ask children to share what they know about rainbows. To guide the discussion, ask:

◎ When do you usually see rainbows?

◎ How do you think a rainbow is made?

◎ What colors do you remember seeing in rainbows?

◎ What would you like to learn about rainbows?

Record children's responses on chart paper.

3 Let children know that they will be making a rainbow right in their classroom. To organize this activity, you may want to either gather as a group or break children into smaller groups and repeat the activity for each group.

4 To make the rainbow, have children follow these steps.

◎ Fill the jar with water.

◎ Place it in direct sunlight on a windowsill or on a table. The jar should be as close to the edge as possible so that the light passing through it will hit the floor below.

◎ Place a large sheet of white poster board on the part of the floor where the sun is shining through the glass. If a rainbow does not appear, try holding the jar in the direct sunlight over the paper.

5 Invite children's observations about what happens and why. Ask: What colors do you see? Have children record the colors and their order then repeat the process several times. What is the color pattern of the rainbow?

ACTIVITY Extension Make rainbow-colored sun catchers. Give children clear plastic lids (from deli containers) and markers or cellophane in all of the rainbow colors. Let them create rainbow-colored designs by either gluing pieces of cellophane to the lid or by drawing on it with the markers. To hang the finished sun catchers in a window, use a hole punch to make a hole in the rim of the lid. Then thread string or yarn through the hole and knot.

Literature Connection *Tom's Rainbow Walk* by Catherine Anholt (Little, Brown and Company, 1989) tells the story of a boy who can't decide what colors he would like his grandmother to use in a sweater she is knitting for him. As you read this book with children, ask them to guess what they think the sweater will look like when it is finished. For additional projects and experiments that explore rainbows and the properties of light, try *Color and Light* by Barbara Taylor (Franklin Watts, 1990).

Learning Center Link

Invite independent exploration of rainbows and light by displaying prisms, flashlights, and pocket mirrors at the center. How can students use the materials to make rainbows? For inexpensive supplies, try Delta Education, (800) 258-1302, or Edmund Scientific, (609) 547-8880.

Name_____

Mystery Mix-Ups

1. For each color combination, guess what the new color will be. Write it under My Prediction.

2. Mix the colors together to make new colors. Paint some of the new color under My Results. Write the color name.

	MY PREDICTION	**MY RESULTS**
red + blue =	_____	_____
red + yellow =	_____	_____
blue + yellow =	_____	_____

Write new color equations below.
Test them out to see what new colors you make.

	MY PREDICTION	**MY RESULTS**
_____ + _____ =	_____	_____
_____ + _____ =	_____	_____
_____ + _____ =	_____	_____
_____ + _____ =	_____	_____

Colors All Around

From safety signs to changing leaves and camouflage, the activities in this section invite children to explore the functional and magical roles of colors in their world.

BACKGROUND NOTES

This section offers many opportunities to delve deeper into some of the ways colors are used in the world around us. In activity 1, Sign Safety, you may want to go further by exploring sign symbols in other parts of the world.

Sign Safety

Children explore the meaning of colors in signs they see and create colorful school safety signs of their own.

Materials

◎ *Red Light, Green Light* by Margaret Wise Brown (Scholastic, 1992) (optional)

◎ poster board or mural paper

◎ paint, markers, crayons

◎ tape

Teaching the Lesson

1. If possible, introduce the activity by sharing *Red Light, Green Light*. Ask children to look at the book cover and describe what they see. Point out the signpost, where the title appears, and ask: Why do you think the title of the book is here? Invite children to guess what the book is about.

2. After you read the book, talk with children about how the different colors in a traffic light help keep motorists and pedestrians safe. Then have children brainstorm additional safety signs and their colors, such as red stop signs and exit signs, orange and black caution signs, yellow pedestrian-crossing and school zone signs, and black and white railroad crossing and speed limit signs. Ask: Why do you think some signs are always the same color?

3. Invite children to design safety signs for their classroom and school. Begin by brainstorming ideas, such as:

◎ a sign by your art supplies that reminds children to be careful with scissors;

◎ a sign outside of your classroom door that reminds students to walk in the hall;

◎ a sign on the way out to the playground that reminds students to check that their shoes are tied before they go out to play.

4. Divide children into cooperative groups. Have each select a sign to design. You may want to make a sign-design checklist to assist children in the process. Questions to consider include:

◎ What shape will our sign be?

◎ What color will get people's attention?

◎ Do we want to have words and pictures? Just pictures? Just words?

◎ Where is the best place to hang our sign?

5. Invite children to present several design ideas and sketches to the class before developing one into a finished sign.

6. When children are satisfied with their work, take a sign-posting expedition around your school.

7. Invite a representative from your local department of transportation or a police officer to take a tour of the safety signs and to talk to children about safety.

ACTIVITY Extension Play a game of red light, green light. Since this game requires a good deal of space, you may want to play outdoors or in a gymnasium. Begin by choosing one child to be the traffic light. The rest of the children can be cars. Have the cars line up shoulder to shoulder at one end of the play area. Have the traffic light stand at the opposite end of the play area with his or her back to the cars. The game begins when the traffic light shouts "green light!" At this command, the cars walk toward the traffic light. To stop the cars, the traffic light turns around and shouts "red light." At this command, the cars must freeze. If the traffic light catches a car moving, he or she can send that car back to the starting line. To resume play, the traffic light turns his or her back to the cars again and says "green light." Can the cars make it to the traffic light without moving on a red light?

Literature Connection *I Read Signs* by Tana Hoban (Greenwillow, 1983) is illustrated with photos of common signs. After reading the book with children, take a sign hunt around your school neighborhood. How many of the signs can students spot? What does each mean?

Learning Center Link

Make traffic lights out of empty milk cartons. Start by having children paint the cartons black. Once the paint dries, they can paint red, yellow, and green circles on each panel then write the words stop, go, and slow on slips of paper and glue each next to the corresponding color. Tie a line of yarn or string from one end of the classroom to another and suspend the children's traffic lights.

SCIENCE

Leaves Change Colors

Children observe the changes in leaves from summer to autumn and create their own leaves for trees in each season.

Note: *Though changes in leaf color may be most dramatic in the northeastern areas of the United States, you can observe changes anywhere there are deciduous trees.*

Materials

◎ mural paper

◎ leaf patterns (see page 31)

◎ 1-inch squares of tissue paper (green, orange, yellow, red, brown)

◎ glue

◎ tape

SCIENCE NOTES

Chlorophyll is a special chemical found in leaves. It makes leaves green and gives them the energy they need to make food out of water and carbon dioxide. Leaves act like food factories for a tree. In fall, the factory shuts down. With the cooler temperatures in fall, trees go through changes. They get less sun because the days are shorter. A barrier forms at the base of leaf stems. This blocks off water and nutrients that normally reach the tree through its leaves. The leaf can then no longer make food. The chlorophyll begins to break down. This exposes other leaf pigments under the green. These pigments produce the shades of red, orange, and yellow we see in autumn.

Teaching the Lesson

1. On two sheets of mural paper draw large tree outlines with empty branches. Display each tree side by side on a wall or bulletin board. Label one of the trees Summer Tree and the other Fall Tree.

2. Show children a picture of a tree in summer. Then show them a picture of a tree with autumn leaves. Invite children to compare the two pictures and make observations about the leaves. Ask children what they know about leaves changing color. Follow up by providing as much detail about the process as your students are ready for. (See Science Notes, left.)

3. Give children copies of the leaf patterns. Ask them to use the tissue paper and glue to make summer and autumn leaves.

4. Have children cut out their leaves then take turns matching their leaves to each tree and gluing or taping them onto the branches. To complete the cycle, discuss what the tree would look like in winter and spring. Let children work in groups , too, to make these trees.

ACTIVITY Extension Go on a leaf hunt, collecting samples as you go. Take along plenty of crayons, colored pencils, markers, and pads of paper to record all the colors you see. How many shades of yellow and green can students spot? What other colors do leaves come in this time of year? Back in the classroom, create a display with the samples or students' drawings, arranging leaves in color families.

Literature Connection Conclude the activity by sharing *Down Come the Leaves* by Henrietta Bancroft (Thomas Y. Crowell, 1961). Through the eyes of two children, this wonderful book provides simple explanations of what happens to trees in autumn.
Sky Tree, by Thomas Locker (HarperCollins, 1995) offers another look at the changes of a tree, combining magnificent paintings with simple, scientific explanations of one tree's changes throughout the seasons. Children may be inspired to adopt their own tree and record with words and pictures what they observe over time.

Learning Center Link

Display fresh leaves, paper, crayons, and other materials for these assorted activities.

◎ *Make leaf rubbings by placing a piece of paper on top of a leaf and rubbing gently with crayons.*

◎ *Use leaves as stencils: place a leaf on a piece of paper (roll up a piece of tape and use it to hold the leaf in place) and paint or color over and around the leaf. Sprinkle salt on the paint for an unusual effect. Let dry overnight, then gently peel away the leaf.*

◎ *Sort leaves by patterns and shapes. (This is a good time to introduce the vocabulary* smooth, lobed, wavy, *and* toothed, *words scientists sometimes use to classify leaves. Have children use pictures and words to record their own sorting methods too.)*

◎ *Use a tree guidebook to match leaves with tree names.*

Note: After introducing the activities to children, you might want to make simple signs that remind children of each activity.

Color Hide-and-Seek

Children play a color hide-and-seek game to observe how animals use color to camouflage themselves from predators.

Materials

◎ tricolored dried pasta shapes; about 25 pieces of each color (yarn in different colors, cut into 1/2-inch pieces, works well too)

◎ 4 chairs

◎ string

SCIENCE NOTES

How well-camouflaged do you think a giraffe is, with its characteristic long neck? Students may be surprised to learn that, giraffes' distinctive coloration, against a sunlit background, helps them blend in to their surroundings quite well. Like giraffes, butterflies and fish also blend into the landscape patterns around them.

Camouflage helps animals hide from their enemies. (It helps some predators hide from their prey too.) Animals that change color to camouflage themselves include chameleons, copperhead snakes, fish, and many kinds of frogs and toads. Some animals that live in cooler parts of the world change colors with each season. The snowshoe hare is one of them. It is white in winter and brown in summer. Can students guess why?

Teaching the Lesson

1. On a grassy area, mark off a large square. Position a chair in each corner and suspend the string between them. For best results, make each side of the square approximately 20 feet long.

2. Scatter the pasta or yarn around the ground inside the square.

3. To play, have small groups of children take turns pretending they are birds searching for worms and other goodies to eat. (The pasta or yarn pieces are the worms.) Challenge them to find as many worms as they can in 30 seconds. Record the colors each pair finds then scatter the worms again and let the next group go.

4. After everyone has had a turn, have children combine and graph their data to see how many of each color they found. Ask: Which colors were easiest to find? Which ones were difficult to find? Why do you think some colors are easier to find?

5. Follow up by inviting children to explain how they think some animals can use their colors to hide themselves from their enemies. Introduce the word *camouflage,* then select some facts from Science Notes (see page 27) to share with children.

ACTIVITY Extension Take the topic further by investigating other kinds of camouflage, including shape and texture (like the walking stick) and warning coloration (like the skunk's distinctive stripe).

Learning Center Link

Let children create camouflage paintings. They can begin by painting or coloring a background environment for an animal then create an animal that will blend into the background. If you have wallpaper samples, children can use them to create their camouflage pictures, cutting out shapes and placing them against a wallpaper background of the same pattern.

Literature Connection Offer a selection of books on camouflage as reference materials as students work on their camouflage pictures.

Camouflage: Nature's Defense by Nancy Warren Ferrell (Franklin Watts, 1989)

I See Animals Hiding by Jim Aronsky (Scholastic, 1995)

Animals and Their Hiding Places by Jane R. McCauley (National Geographic, 1986)

Animal Camouflage: Hide and Seek Animals by Janet McDonnel (Child's World, 1990)

Make a Mini-Book

Share a Native American tale about butterflies, one of nature's most colorful creatures.

Note: *How the Butterflies Got Their Colors is an adaptation of a tale told by the Papago (Pah'-pah-g`o) Indians. Most members of the Papago, which means "bean people," reside in their traditional homeland, which is the dry Southern Arizona desert. Despite their dry living conditions, the Papago became skilled farmers. They developed primitive reservoirs to collect water that overflowed from summer storms. This enabled them to grow maize, cotton, and beans. The central character in the story is the Papago's Elder brother or Creator.*

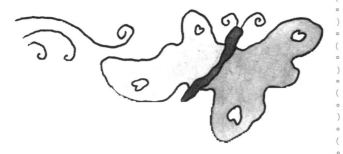

Materials

◎ *How Butterflies Got Their* Colors reproducible mini-book (see page 32)

◎ stapler

◎ scissors

◎ crayons

Teaching the Lesson

1 Make a copy of the reproducible mini-book for each child.

2 Assist children in cutting out the pages and assembling the book. Staple along the left side to hold the pages together.

3 Read the story aloud as children follow along in their own books.

4 Once children are familiar with the story, they can add illustrations on each page. Allow children several opportunities to revisit the story by re-reading it in pairs or groups. Let children bring their books home to share with their families too.

ACTIVITY Extension Just like the man in the story, children can create butterflies out of materials. Buttons, felt, scrap paper, yarn, fabric, and glitter and tissue paper are just some of the materials they might like to use. Let children write and tell their own stories about how their butterflies got their color.

Literature Connection *Greedy Zebra* by Mwenge Hadithi (Little, Brown and Company, 1984) tells how the first animals spruce up their dull colors after they discover a cave full of furs, skins, horns, and tails. The greedy zebra arrives late and acquires his stripes in a very humorous way. Follow up by changing the end of the story. Instead of a zebra, have another animal arrive late. How does this animal acquire his or her colors?

Learning
Center Link

Display books and fact cards about butterflies so children can discover more about them.

If possible, raise a caterpillar in a covered aquarium tank so children can observe its transformation into a butterfly. The following companies have affordable kits available that contain larvae, food, and instructions.

Carolina Biological Company
(Raise-A-Butterfly Kit)
2700 York Rd.
Burlington, NC 27215
(800) 334-5551

Delta Education, Inc.
(Butterfly Garden Kit)
P.O. Box 3000
Nashua, NH 03061-3000
(800) 442-5444

Leaf Patterns

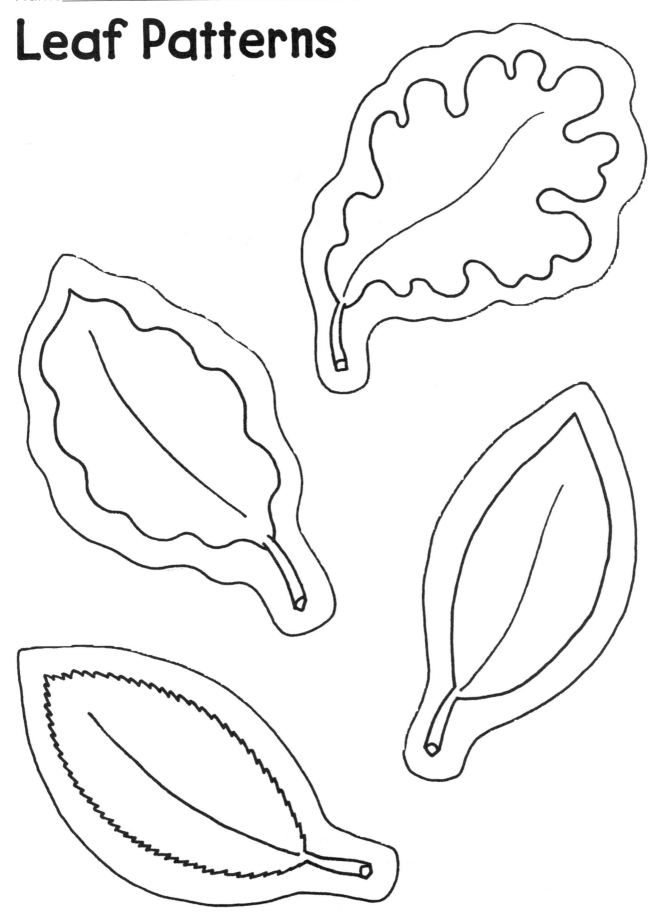

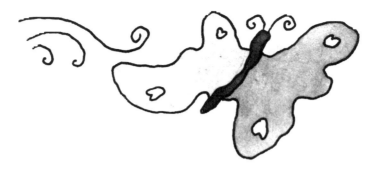

How Butterflies Got Their Colors

A Story of the Papago Indians

Illustrated by _____

One late summer day, an old man was out for a walk.
He saw children playing in fields of bright blue, red, white, and
yellow flowers.

The man sat under a tall tree with deep green leaves to watch.
He began to think about how the days would soon turn cold.

3

The trees and flowers would go to sleep for the winter.
This made the man sad. He would miss their beautiful colors.
"How could I save the colors?" he wondered.

4

Suddenly he had an idea.
He put some colorful leaves and flower petals into a bag.

5

He added green pine needles, golden sunlight, and bird songs.
Then he called the children over and gave them the bag.

6

When the children opened the bag, butterflies of every color flew out.
The butterflies danced and sang.

7

Then along came some birds who said, "The songs belong to us!"
The man agreed and gave the songs back to the birds.
Since that day, colorful butterflies still dance as they fly.
Now they just do it very quietly.

8

Colors Go to Work

Who uses colors? Artists, mapmakers, and bakers all use color in their work. So do landscapers, architects, car-makers, sign-makers, and other kinds of workers. With the activities in this section, children explore some of the ways people use color in their work, and gain an appreciation of the way colors and careers connect.

Meet an Artist

Introduce students to Vincent van Gogh, a painter who is known for his use of color and the feelings they help convey. Then let them experiment with the thick, colorful paints he used to create their own works of art.

Materials

◎ selected van Gogh works (as mentioned in Art Notes, right; you might check with your school and local library for art history books that contain van Gogh's work; a gallery or poster shop may also have posters and postcards available)

◎ soap flake paint (see recipe, below)

◎ 8 1/2-by-11-inch writing paper (divided in half vertically)

◎ squeeze bottles or resealable sandwich bags

◎ craft sticks

◎ paintbrushes

◎ paper plates

◎ water color paper (or finger-paint paper or freezer paper)

SOAP-FLAKE PAINT

◎ 2 cups soap flakes

◎ 1 cup water

◎ 4 tablespoons dry tempera powder (red, blue, yellow)

Mix ingredients thoroughly and store in squeeze bottles. Or try using resealable sandwich bags to hold each color of paint. Spoon about three tablespoons of paint into one of the bottom corners of a bag. Seal the bag and snip off a small piece of the paint-filled corner. Children can squeeze the paint onto paper-plate palettes the way they would with squeeze bottles.

ART NOTES

Vincent van Gogh had a special way of using color to express his feelings. Van Gogh's first paintings were of the poor farmers and coal miners (The Potato Eaters), who he worked hard to help. He used very thick, dark, muddy-colored oil paints and heavy brush strokes in these paintings. Van Gogh would often mix and apply his paints with a palette knife (a knife with a thin, flexible blade) instead of a brush.

Later in his life, van Gogh moved to Paris, France, where he met many artists. Some, called Impressionists, were interested in showing how the colors of nature looked in sunlight. They did this by painting many light brush strokes of bright, clear colors next to each other. Van Gogh liked their style of painting. It made him feel happy and excited about his own work. Soon he started using bright colors (Self Portrait with a Straw Hat).

Later, van Gogh moved to the country, where he found beautiful flowers, bright sunshine, and clear blue skies. He wanted to paint everything he saw (The Bedroom at Arles). Van Gogh set up a studio in a little yellow house and spent his days painting the flowers in the sunny fields (Still Life with Sunflowers).

Teaching the Lesson

1. Share pictures of some of Vincent van Gogh's paintings with children. Invite their observations about his use of color.

2. Explain to children that they will be using thick, colorful paints like van Gogh did to create their own paintings. Prepare the children by taking them on a walk outside on a sunny day. Ask them to look for elements in nature that they would like to paint. Children can list items on the left-hand side of the divided paper and record corresponding colors on the right.

3. When children are ready to paint, distribute paper plates, paper, brushes, and craft sticks. Have children use their lists from the walk to select paint colors, squeezing paint onto paper-plate palettes then returning to their work spaces. Demonstrate how to use the craft sticks and brushes to pick up paints from the palette and mix them on another paper plate.

4. Have children create information cards about their work to display with their paintings. These cards can include their name, birth date, name of painting, and a few sentences about the painting.

5. Display the paintings and information cards in a classroom art gallery. Encourage children to browse the gallery and compare and contrast their work with van Gogh's.

ACTIVITY Extension Visit a local art museum or gallery with children so they can get a closer look at art. Try some or all of the following ideas to enhance the visit:

1. Create a treasure hunt of items that children can look for during their visit. Items could range from a sculpture to a tree in a painting.

2. Share stories about the artists whose work children will see.

3. Give children paper and pencils to take along so they can sketch as they go.

4. Find out if the museum or gallery can organize an art project for your class.

5. Ask children to choose a piece of art that they like or dislike. Invite them to discuss why they feel the way they do about the piece.

Literature Connection Books to enhance your focus on color and art include:

Van Gogh by Ernest Raboff (HarperTrophy, 1988). Learn about the artist's life and take a close look at 15 of his paintings.

Beside the Bay by Sheila White Samton (Philomel Books, 1987). Take a closer look at nature's colors.

Painting the Wind: A Story of Vincent van Gogh by Michelle Dionetti (Little, Brown, 1996). A visit with van Gogh inspires a young girl to paint her own pictures filled with the same glorious colors that characterize this artist's work.

Learning Center Link

Art can be a very positive and helpful way for children to express themselves. This fun and challenging game will encourage children's self expression.

TO PLAY:

1. Write the following lists on chart paper.

Feelings

happy	mad
sad	friendly
nice	mean
brave	scared

Characters

dog	child
baby	mother
friend	father
sister	brother
teacher	fish
cat	bird

Places

forest	house
ocean	classroom
mountains	playground
birthday party	

Time and Weather

night	day
snowy	rainy
cloudy	sunny
windy	foggy

2. Ask children to choose one word from each list and paint a picture that shows all of the elements they selected.

Color My World

Children discover how mapmakers use color in their work.

Materials

◎ maps (local, state, world, building, park, bus routes, subway, and so on)

◎ chalkboard or chart paper

◎ paint, markers, crayons

◎ butcher paper

Teaching the Lesson

1. Display a variety of maps. Children might like to share some from home too. Ask children what they know about how maps are used. Encourage them to talk about times they've seen people using maps—maybe parents planning a trip, tourists trying to find their way around, weather reporters on the news telling what's happening and where, and so on.

2. Locate a map key. Ask: How do you think mapmakers use color to represent landmarks such as water, trees, and mountains?

3 Draw an outline of your classroom on a piece of butcher paper. Explain that this is how the classroom's shape would look to a bird flying over it. Invite children to imagine that they are birds. What do they see? Together, create a key that uses different colors to represent various objects. Bookshelves may be blue, desks may be brown, tables may be orange, windows may be yellow, and so on. Have children fill in objects on the map, drawing simple shapes such as squares, rectangles, and circles to represent objects, and shading them in using the key as a guide.

4 Display the map then use it to play a follow-the-directions game. For example, ask children to use the color key to locate the bookshelves. Then ask them to turn right and tell you what object they find.

ACTIVITY Extension Take children for a walk around the school neighborhood or play area. Give each child a note pad and pencil to draw or write about roads and landmarks they see. When you return to the classroom, let children use their drawings and notes to create maps. You may want to try making three-dimensional maps. Children can design a key and use objects such as egg cartons, milk cartons, and bathroom tissue tubes to represent landmarks, then paint them to correspond to the key. As a fun take-home component, children can create maps of their bedrooms.

Literature Connection Enrich your mapmaking activities with these books:

The Whole World in Your Hands: Looking at Maps by Melvin Berger and Gilda Berger (Ideals Children's Books, 1993). A simple introduction to maps.

As the Crow Flies by Gail Hartman (Bradbury Press, 1991). Hop, gallop, and soar through different geographical areas with a rabbit, a horse, a crow, and a gull.

Learning Center Link

Display a variety of maps for children to explore. Suggest that children notice ways colors are used on these maps.

LANGUAGE ARTS/ART

Bake Me a Cake

Students discover how color and cakes go together.

Materials

◎ reproducible cake pattern (see page 43)

◎ sturdy paper

◎ scissors

◎ paint, markers, crayons, pencils

◎ glitter

◎ colored paper

◎ glue

◎ cookbooks

◎ food magazines

Teaching the Lesson

1 Plan a visit to a bakery or invite a baker to visit the classroom and demonstrate his or her cake-baking art. If neither of these options is possible, you can show children pictures of cakes in magazines and

then decorate them to create their own works of art. For a twist, use food coloring to tint white frosting. Children can use clean paintbrushes to paint edible pictures on their crackers. (Hint: Mini-muffin tins make great containers for this activity. Just place papers in muffin-tin cups, add white frosting, and tint each section a different color. Lift the papers out for easy cleanup.)

cookbooks. Compare an undecorated cake to a frosted cake, a child's birthday cake to a wedding cake. Ask the baker to talk with children about how different colors and kinds of icing are created and why color is important in decorating a cake.

2   When you return to class, distribute the reproducible patterns, sturdy paper, pencils, and scissors for children to trace and cut out their cakes. Children might also choose to create their own cake shapes. Invite children to dictate or write a sentence about how their cakes look before they add color.

3   Let children use markers, crayons, paint, colored construction paper, glitter, glue, and other materials to decorate their cakes. When cakes are complete, ask children to dictate or write another sentence describing their decorating decisions.

4   Display decorated cakes on a bulletin board with children's before and after sentence strips. To enhance the display, add a baker's hat, pictures of mixing bowls and spoons, as well as a fun heading.

ACTIVITY Extension   Children can transfer their cake-decorating skills to graham cracker cakes. Provide graham crackers, white frosting, tubes of icing, and colored sprinkles. Children can frost their graham crackers

Literature Connection   The following books will inspire children's cake decorating art:

My First Baking Book by Helen Drew (Knopf Books for Young Readers, 1991)

The Bake-a-Cake Book: Beat the Batter, Measure the Flour, Bake a Cake with the Cake Bakers by Marie Meijer (Chronicle, 1994)

Learning Center Link

Set up a bakery for dramatic play. Stock the center with colorful play clay, rolling pins, mixing bowls and spoons, pie plates, mini-muffin tins, cookie cutters, aprons, chef hats, pretend money, and a cash register.

Name_____

Celebrate Colors!

Children wrap up their color investigations with a celebration that lets parents and other guests share in their accomplishments. Plans for activities, games, and goodies follow.

PART 1: Design Invitations

Students work in teams to create colorful invitations for guests.

Materials

- construction paper
- plain paper
- assorted art supplies
- glue
- scissors

1 Have children work in groups to create invitations that represent the theme *Colors*. Help groups decide on an approach by reviewing favorite activities. For example, one group might like to create invitations that feature van Gogh-like art. Another might like to picture colorful rainbows or butterflies. A third might like to create pictures of masterful cakes on the invitations.

2 Decide on the information each invitation needs to include, then copy it on chart paper and post several copies around the room for easy reference.

3 Have children combine art and information on invitations then deliver (or assist in addressing envelopes for invitations that need to be mailed).

Note: *Keep track of the number of invitations sent out and responses that come in each day. For a quick math activity, ask children to determine how many more people still need to respond.*

PART 2: Make Party Banners

Let each group design a panel that when pieced together with other panels will result in a giant banner to decorate your classroom for the big day.

Materials

- butcher paper
- assorted art supplies (markers, paint, crayons, fabric scraps and other collage materials, and so on)
- scissors
- glue
- tape

1 Give each group a section of butcher paper to create a panel of the banner. Have groups transfer their invitation designs from Part 1 to the banner panels.

2 Work with children to tape completed panels together and display.

PART 3: The Big Day

From projects and activities to games and goodies, here are some suggestions for planning a memorable celebration.

STUDENTS LEAD THE WAY

Build time into your celebration to let children share theme projects and activities with their guests. If students have been storing work in a portfolio, have them take time before the celebration to organize their work and select some of the pieces they are most proud of to share. Let children lead guests in some of their favorite activities from the unit too. For example:

- play a game of red light, green light (see page 24)
- survey and graph guests' eye color and compare to students' original findings (see page 10)
- survey and graph guests' favorite colors and compare with the class results (see page 16)

- ◎ create colorful paintings like van Gogh (see page 38)

- ◎ give guided tours of students' colorful school safety signs (see page 24)

- ◎ play color hide-and-seek (see page 27)

- ◎ challenge guests to solve students' Colors Scavenger Hunt riddles (see page 12)

CUT AND COLOR

Set up materials for making colorful head bands at your learning center. Post directions so that guests can assist children.

Materials

- ◎ a measuring tape

- ◎ construction paper

- ◎ scissors

- ◎ stapler

- ◎ glue

- ◎ assorted art supplies (such as markers, crayons, tissue paper, glitter)

1. Measure around the top of your child's head, about one inch above the eyes. Add one inch to this length.

2. Place the tape measure on the construction paper and mark off the length. Measure and mark a width of about three inches.

3. Have your child cut out the headband strip and decorate with a colorful pattern.

4. Ask your child to write his or her name on the back of the strip. Staple the ends of the strip together to make a headband.

COLLABORATIVE COLLAGES

Invite children and guests to create collaborative rainbow collages modeled after the cover of this book. Provide assorted art materials (such as crayons, markers, colored paper, scissors) as well as magazines (for cutting out pictures). Each child and a guest can work together to create a section of a rainbow, using pictures of objects that represent that color. For example, to create the red band of the rainbow, one team might picture a slice of watermelon, a fire truck, a setting sun, a cardinal, red tulips, and a bunch of radishes. Have each team arrange its art in the shape of a rainbow, one arc above another.

A PLAY TO PERFORM

Use the retelling of the story *How Butterflies Got Their Color* (see pages 32–35) to write a play for children to perform. Design a simple set together (for example, making a mural that pictures the field of flowers and the tree), assign parts (the main character, butterflies, birds, children in the field), and rehearse before performing for guests.

PASS THE ORANGE

In this version of a favorite relay, everyone wins! You'll need oranges (one per team) and a chair. To set up the game, clear a playing space in the room. Divide players into equal teams. Line up the teams side by side at one end of the room. Place a chair at the opposite end of the room from each team. Give an orange to the person who is first in line for each team.

To play, have team members take turns walking to the chair and back with an orange between their knees. The next player in line repeats the process. This continues until everyone has had a chance to go.

LITERATURE SHARE

Display assorted literature from the unit for parents to share with children. Guests might like to spend time quietly sharing a story with a child or two or reading aloud for the whole group. Though children will have heard the story before, re-reading allows them to revisit vocabulary and become more familiar with the content, making new connections along the way. For a twist, let your young readers read aloud to their guests.

RAINBOW KABOBS

Guests and children work together to make a healthy and colorful treat to eat.

Materials

◎ bamboo kabob sticks (available in many grocery stores and in kitchen supply stores)

◎ fresh fruit in rainbow colors (for example, red: strawberries; orange: orange sections; yellow: pineapple; green: kiwi; blue: blueberries; purple: purple grapes)

◎ plastic knives (you may want to have a knife with a steel blade for hard-to-cut fruits)

◎ cutting boards

◎ bowls

◎ paper plates

◎ napkins

Note: *Plan ahead for this activity by asking parents to bring cutting boards the day of the party if they can. (If you're short on cutting boards, paper plates will do.) The day of the party, prewash the fruit.*

1. Pair children and guests and give each a set of materials (one bamboo stick per person, a couple of plastic knives, a cutting board, and a paper plate each).

2. Have each team cut up a couple of pieces of fruit into small chunks. Place fruit in bowls and arrange buffet-style on a table with paper plates and napkins.

3. Invite children and guests to choose fruits they would like to build their rainbow kabobs.

WRAP-UP

After the party, invite children to reflect on the unit. What did they like best? Do they have memorable moments to share? Let them write or dictate responses then illustrate. Put students' illustrated responses together to create a scrapbook of your unit on colors. Use photo corners (available at photography, stationery, and craft stores) to add photographs from your celebration and other activities.